LET'S DRAW
PEOPLE

Reycraft Books
55 Fifth Avenue
New York, NY 10003

reycraftbooks.com

Reycraft Books is a trade imprint and trademark of Newmark Learning, LLC.

Library of Congress Control Number: 2022914958

Hardcover ISBN: 978-1-4788-7613-7
Paperback ISBN: 978-1-4788-7614-4

Photo Credits: Inside Back Jacket B, Page 3A: subjug/Getty Images; Book Spine, Jacket Spine: pixhook/
Getty Images; Page ii, iii, iv: handsomepictures/Shutterstock; Page 5: Photograph by Stephen Kennedy;
Page 7: Courtesy of Kyle Beckett; Page 9: Courtesy of. Huan-Hong Wu; Page 11: ;Page 13: Courtesy of Colin
Bootman; Page 15: Courtesy of Sina Nayeri; Page 17: Courtesy of Javier RamÃrez; Page 19,21: Courtesy of
Núria Munné; Page 23: ;Page 25: Courtesy of Wook Jin Jung; Page 27: ; Page 29: ;
All other images from Shutterstock

Printed in Dongguan, China. 8557/0922/19555

10 9 8 7 6 5 4 3 2 1

First Edition published by Reycraft Books 2023.

Reycraft Books and Newmark Learning, LLC support diversity and
the First Amendment, and celebrate the right to read.

LET'S DRAW PEOPLE!

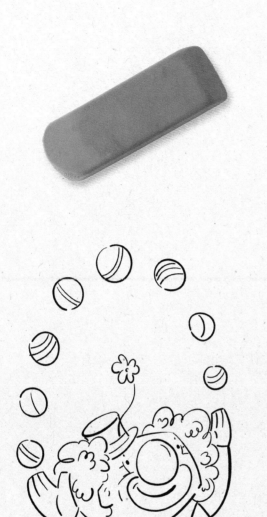

Thirteen of your favorite illustrators have come together to help make drawing people a little easier. Drawing should be fun! Everyone has their own style, so don't forget—there's no need to be perfect! So if you make a mistake, don't worry. Erase or start fresh on a new piece of paper. It takes a lot of practice to become an artist, so keep at it and eventually you'll draw just the way you want!

Every artist has their own special way of working. Some start with a pencil sketch on paper and color it with paint or markers. Others use a computer or tablet with a stylus to make their drawings. Some use both. Use what you have and what feels right. The options are endless! Combining different methods and materials can often produce beautiful and unexpected results. There are no rules when being creative. Give in to your imagination. Study the artists' step-by-step directions, try their helpful tips, and get started. Are you ready? Let's draw people!

LET'S DRAW A KID RUNNING . . .

1.

2.

3.

4.

5.

6.

TIPS AND TRICKS...

✔ Don't get so hung up on the proportions. Variation is a great way to add your unique style.

✔ A consistent light source helps give the character more dimension and life.

LET'S DRAW EXPRESSIONS . . .

1. HAPPY

2. SILLY

3. SAD

4. SCARED

5. WORRIED

6. CONFUSED

7. ANGRY

8. SNEAKY

KYLE BECKETT

TIPS AND TRICKS...

✔ Eyebrows are extremely expressive, and they don't have to match each other!

✔ Bigger eyes or a smaller mouth can change everything.

LET'S DRAW A BIKER . . .

1. Draw the head, body, and arms.

Note that the back arm is longer.

2. Draw your favorite hairstyle. Remember the wind is blowing!

3. Give her a seat and two wheels. The wheels are about the size of a head.

4. Go ahead and finish the bike.

6. Add a backpack and decorations to the dress and you're done!

5. Don't forget the leg in the back!

LIAN AN-LIN

LET'S DRAW A CLOWN . . .

1.

2.

3.

4.

5.

6.

7.

8.

TIM PALIN

TIPS AND TRICKS...

✔ Give those clothes some flair. Add polka dots or tiger stripes! Sometimes, the clothes make the clown.

✔ Mess around with the clown's face make-up. Rosy cheeks can be stars. The big, painted-on mouth can be a tiny little heart shape. Add big, fancy eyelashes if you like! When it comes to a clown face, personality is everything!

LET'S DRAW A PIRATE . . .

1.

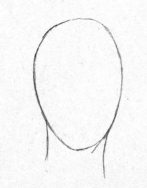

2.

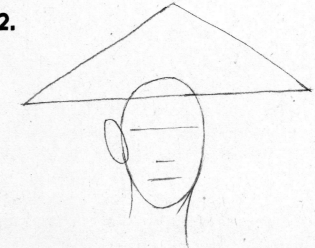

3.

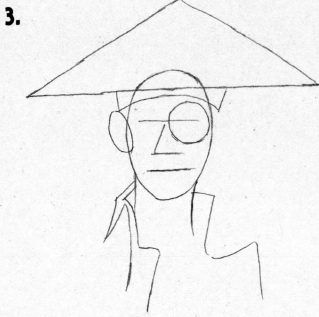

4.

5.

6.

TIPS AND TRICKS...

✔ At the beginning of each drawing, make sure your pencil strokes are light. A light drawing allows you to easily correct mistakes over time.

✔ Start your drawing by using shapes that you are already familiar with. Common shapes are circles, triangles, rectangles, straight lines, curved lines, and angled lines.

LET'S DRAW A GRANDMA . . .

1.

2.

3.

4.

5.

6.

TIPS AND TRICKS...

✔ Look at your grandma to get inspired. My grandma loves pink!

✔ It's easier to draw the shape of the grandma's head first, then her face. Finally, you can add the body and be creative with her personality.

LET'S DRAW A NINJA . . .

1.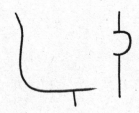

2.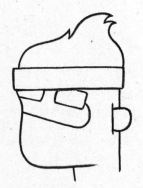

3.

4.

5.

6.

SR. RENY

TIPS AND TRICKS...

✔ Use darker colors for the right side. The ninja will look like he is coming out of the page.

✔ Add lines to create the folds in the clothes. It will be a more realistic ninja.

LET'S DRAW BOYS' HAIRCUTS . . .

1.

2.

3.

4.

5.

6.

7.

8.

9.

10.

11.

12.

ÁNGELES RUIZ

TIPS AND TRICKS...

✔ Use a color pencil with its point worn out to create waves for the curly hair or straight lines for the straight hair.

✔ Spread the hair into 3 areas: the bangs, the right side, and the left side. Then repeat the hair lines from each area in the same direction.

✔ Invent haircuts and pretend to be a hairstylist.

LET'S DRAW GIRLS' HAIRCUTS . . .

1.

2.

3.

4.

5.

6.

7.

8.

9.

10.

11.

12.

ÁNGELES RUIZ

TIPS AND TRICKS...

✔ To do the hair, you can use a color pencil with the sharp point already worn out. Draw lines following the same direction. You can also draw an outline and fill it with a color.

✔ Bigger puffs of hair, longer braids, or whatever exaggerated thing you make up will add a unique feature to your character.

LET'S DRAW A SUPERHERO . . .

1.

2.

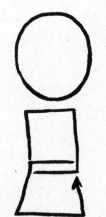

3.

4.

5.

6.

7.

8.

9.

CHUCK GONZALES

TIPS AND TRICKS...

✔ Always start with a light sketch so you can figure out the basic shapes of the figure before making darker lines.

✔ Highlights can make drawings and paintings pop. Put highlights at the highest point of an object where the light would hit it.

LET'S DRAW A ROBOT . . .

1.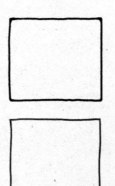

2.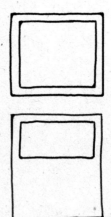

3.

4.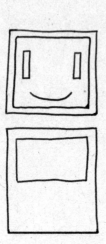

5.

6.

7.

8.

WOOK JIN JUNG

TIPS AND TRICKS...

✔ It's all about rectangles and squares! Drawing a robot is the same as making it with toy blocks. Draw different sizes of rectangles and see how you can put them together into a robot shape.

✔ This robot's body and head are very stiff. However, its legs and arms are very flexible and elastic. Try to draw them in any way you like!

LET'S DRAW A WIZARD . . .

1.

2.

3.

4.

5.

6.

MARTIN ONTIVEROS

TIPS AND TRICKS...

✔ Wizards don't tend to cut their hair much, so the longer you draw it, the better. Especially the beard.

✔ Wizards dress to impress. They like to wear flowing robes and tall hats. You can color them as fun as you want and add whatever symbols you like.

LET'S DRAW AN ASTRONAUT . . .

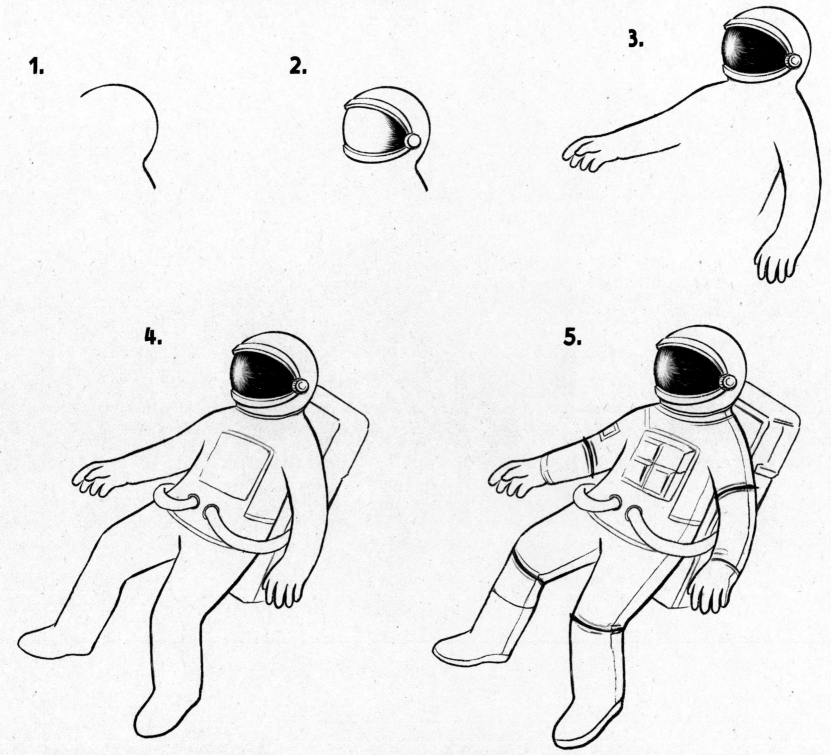

1.

2.

3.

4.

5.

6.

VIRGINIA MORI

TIPS AND TRICKS...

✔ Don't forget to draw the shadows on one side of the character. That will allow for a more realistic image and make it look 3D.

✔ You can paint a blue sky full of stars in the background to create a deep atmosphere!

LET'S DRAW A SNEAKER . . .

1.

2.

3.

4.

5.

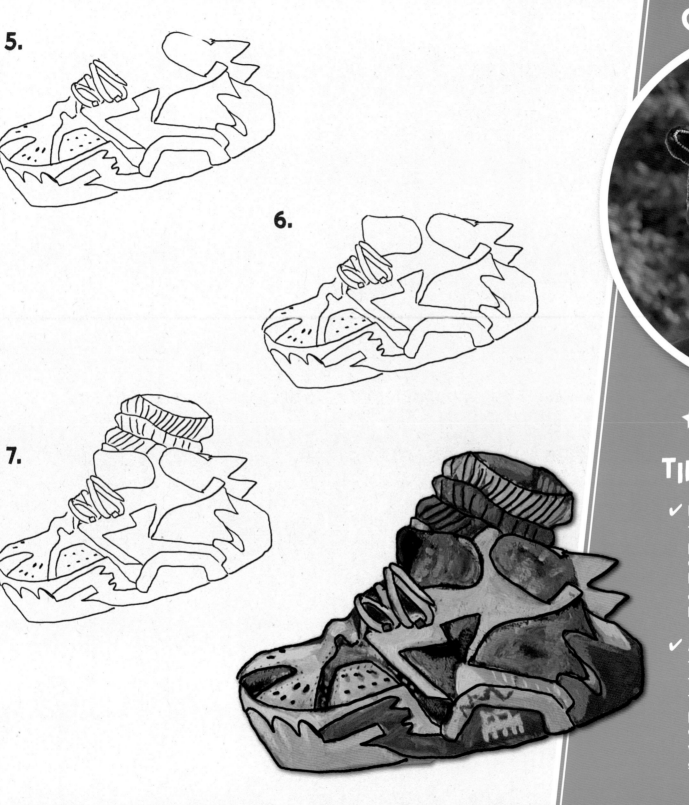

6.

7.

C.G. ESPERANZA

TIPS AND TRICKS...

✔ Don't be afraid to trace the drawing using tracing paper on top of this demonstration. Tracing will help you understand the drawing better by showing how the lines connect.

✔ Afterwards, try drawing the sneaker by observing these steps without tracing. Then after a few practice drawings, try drawing it from memory without looking at these steps.

Be sure to check out all these other titles from Reycraft Books, illustrated by the artists from *Let's Draw People!*

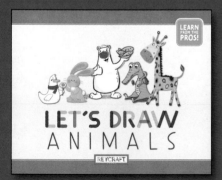